Combat History Series
The Civil War

The Irish Brigade

By Steven J. Wright

Steven Wright Publishing
A Wright/Grenadier Production

Acknowledgements

As with all projects of this nature, assistance and support from many people brought this book to fruition.

Professional gratitude and appreciation is extended to Michael J. McAfee, Curator, U.S. Military Academy Museum, West Point; J. Craig Nannos, Historian, Tom DuClos, of the New York Division of Military and Naval Affairs; Earl "Jerry" Coates for his assistance in research with uniforms and accouterments; the U.S. Army Military History Institute at Carlisle Barracks; and all of my colleagues at The Civil War Library and Museum.

Pat Purcell, Greg Thorpe, and Jack Tracy showed great skill as photographers. Special thanks to David Hann for the use of artifacts identified to members of the Irish Brigade, to Roger Hunt and Ken Powers for the use of photographs and John Genovese for his technical advice.

Finally, heartfelt appreciation to so many others who always kept the faith.

——Steven J. Wright

Cover figure, "Standard bearer of the 69th," sculpted courtesy of Andrew Chernak.

Springfield, PA

Color Plates by Raymond Rubin

Dedicated to the memory of M.G.W.

Published 1992 by Steven Wright Publishing
P.O. Box 171
Springfield, PA 19064-0171

A Steven Wright/Grenadier Models Production
©1992 Steven Wright Publishing

Typeset by Blue Light Computer Services, Claymont, DE.
Printed in the United States of America.

ISBN 1-881683-00-1

Contents

Song of the Irish Brigade

We've never swerved from our old green flag,
Upborne o'er many a bloody plain;
'Tis now a torn and tattered rag,
But we will bear it proudly oft again.
We will raise on high, this dear old flag,
From Liffy's bank to Shannon's stream,
'Till victory o'er the pirate rag
Upon our sacred cause shall beam.

CHORUS

Hurrah! Hurrah! for our dear old flag.
Hurrah for our gallant leader, too;
Though 'tis a torn and tattered rag,
We would not change it for the new.

We've borne it with the Stripes and Stars,
From Fair Oaks to Frederick's bloody plain;
And see, my boys, our wounds and scars
Can tell how well we did the same.
Be sure, our chieftain, of his race,
Was ever foremost 'mid the brave,
Where death met heroes face to face,

And gathered harvests for the grave.

CHORUS

We miss full many a comrade's smile,
The grasp of many a friendly hand,
We mourn their loss, and grieve the while
They had not died for fatherland.
But o'er their fresh and gory graves —
We swear it now and evermore —
To free green Erin, land of slaves,
And banish tyrants from her shore

CHORUS

Now we're pledged to free this land,
So long the exile's resting-place;
To crush for aye a traitorus band,
And wipe out treason's deep disgrace.
Then let us pledge Columbia's cause,
God prosper poor old Ireland, too!
We'll trample all the tyrant laws:
Hurrah for the old land and the new!

CHORUS

Written by an unknown soldier of the 63rd New York Infantry Regiment.

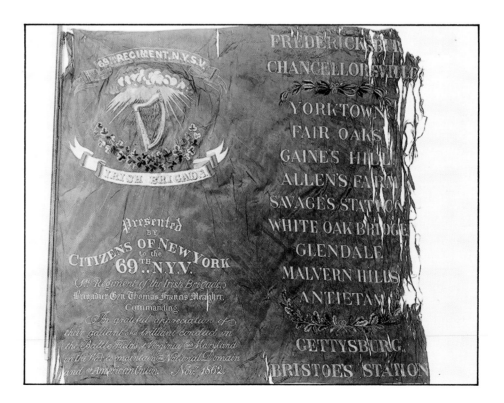

Second-model Irish flag carried by the 69th New York Infantry. *Courtesy of Ken Powers.*

Introduction

They were volunteer soldiers, with names like Cavanaugh, Flynn, Kelly, Murphy, O'Sullivan, and Shea. If given the opportunity to answer why they chose to fight for their adopted land, they might say to preserve the Union, for money or adventure, or to extend freedom to those who were enslaved. As Irish immigrants or descendents of Irish ancestors, the concept of freedom was not an abstract thought.

They rallied at the chance to show their dedication and love for their new country. Proud of their past and of what their future held, they carried into battle a green silk flag with a golden harp alongside the flag of their adopted nation. Their blood was spilled at places like Fair Oaks, Malvern Hill, Antietam, Fredericksburg, Chancellorsville, Gettysburg, the Wilderness, Spotsylvania, Petersburg, Deep Bottom, Reams' Station, Hatcher's Run, Farmville, and Appomattox.

When it was over, when the flags were furled for the last time and the uniforms stored away in trunks in dusty attics, the white-haired veterans would gather to relive their exploits; to talk of fallen comrades, of fights remembered, and of days when they were young. The last man is long since dead, and all that remains are the memories which they have left. But their deeds and sacrifices shall forever live in the hearts of their countrymen.

The purpose of this book is not to provide a history of the Irish Brigade, but instead to honor the contributions and sacrifices of the men who fought beside the green flag of Erin. Although the Civil War ended more than six generations ago, their tales are told in their own words, some being published for the first time.

A Brief History of the Irish Brigade

It would be impossible to determine exactly how many sons of Ireland or their descendents fought for the Union or the Confederacy during the Civil War, but the number would run into the thousands. At least forty Federal units were composed primarily of Irishmen, or had a significant number of Irish within their ranks. The most famous of these regiments composed the Irish Brigade.

Born from the 69th Regiment, New York State Militia, the Brigade was originally composed of the 63rd, 69th, and 88th New York Infantry Regiments. Raised by Thomas Francis Meagher, a former captain in the 69th N.Y.S.M., the brigade was eventually designated the Second Brigade, First Division, Second Army Corps of the Army of the Potomac. During the Peninsula Campaign, in the spring of 1862, the Brigade was strengthened with the temporary assignment of the non-Irish 29th Massachusetts Infantry. In October, 1862, the 116th Pennsylvania Infantry, composed primarily of Irishmen from Philadelphia, was assigned to the brigade. A month later, the 29th Massachusetts was traded to the Ninth Corps for the 28th Massachusetts, another Irish regiment.

Throughout its term of service, the Irish Brigade was almost always at the vanguard, and as a result suffered heavy casualties; whether it be the attack on "Bloody Lane" at the battle of Antietam, the assault against Marye's Heights at Fredericksburg, or the maelstrom of the Wheatfield at Gettysburg. Because of high casualties, efforts were made following the battle of Chancellorsville to disband the brigade. Protesting the threatened dissolution of the brigade, Meagher resigned his commission on May 14, 1863. His resignation was later cancelled, although he never again served in the field with the brigade.

Although the brigade continued to distinguish itself in battle, mounting casualties necessitated changes within the brigade. By the middle of 1864 the brigade had been reduced to nearly regimental strength.

The Irish Brigade was disbanded in June, 1864 when the New York regiments were consolidated into the Third Brigade, First Division, Second Army Corps. The 116th Pennsylvania was transferred to another brigade the following month. Later that year the Second Irish Brigade was created when the 7th New York Heavy Artillery joined the 28th Massachusetts, and the 63rd, 69th, and 88th New York Infantry Regiments. The 4th New York Heavy Artillery replaced the 7th in early 1865. It was in this configuration that the Irish Brigade served throughout the rest of the war.

Thomas Francis Meagher served as the brigade's only commanding general; although Richard Byrnes, Richard Duryea, Patrick Kelly, Robert Nugent, and Thomas Smyth temporarily held the command at various times throughout brigade's existence.

Our flag of the Stars and Stripes was well struck, and the standard-bearer of the dear old Green Flag was shot down; but the flag was instantly raised again."

THE 69TH N.Y.S.M. AT THE BATTLE OF BULL RUN

In the pre-dawn hours of July 21, 1861, the men of the 69th New York State Militia awoke with the knowledge that a great battle, perhaps the only one of the war, was about to be fought.

As part of Brigadier General William T. Sherman's brigade, the regiment marched to the scene of battle that morning, but were held in reserve until 2:30 p.m. when they moved down the Sudley Road toward Henry Hill. The scene on the road gave the men their first look at the sickening horror of war, with hundreds of dead and wounded men lying about, sometimes three or four deep. Thomas Francis Meagher, commander of the 69th, recalled, "Sherman's Brigade was ordered up to relieve the regiments that had been under fire for five hours and more. The 69th led the way, and, as they hurried up the hill, the elasticity and enthusiasm of their race seemed to pervade them thoroughly."

The men of the 69th watched patiently as their comrades were sent against the Confederate defenses. Noticing that the regiment's green flag served as a prominent target for the enemy, Colonel Michael Corcoran asked the standard bearer to withdraw it from the view of the Confederates. "I'll never lower it," replied the color bearer, who was then killed instantly by a rebel bullet.

After watching the vain attempts of the 2nd Wisconsin and 79th New York to push the Confederates from the protection of Henry House Hill, it was finally the turn of the 69th.

The men rose from the protection of the road, formed in company lines, and slowly climbed the slope of the hill, carefully making their way over wounded comrades and broken artillery caissons. In a letter published in *The New York Leader*, a participant of the battle described the beginning of the regiment's attack:

Worn out by our long and quick march, still more so by the fatigue of clearing fences, ditches, and streams, we stopped for a short moment and fired deliberately into the enemy. Then another volley, then another, and we charged up the heights to their battery with all the impetuosity of our race; but we were like 'sheep sent to the slaughter.' The cannon belched forth their shells in our midst, killing our men in groups, and scattering them in all directions. But even they halted, tried to close up, and fired again; and then, just as we seemed to carry our point, we found ourselves fired into on the right flank and rear by the Rebel cavalry, who emerged from the woods and struck down and picked off all the men near them.

Irish Brigade historian Captain D.P. Conyngham recalled the actions of Captain Thomas Francis Meagher:

> *Meagher's company of Zouaves suffered desperately, their red dress making them a conspicuous mark for the enemy. When Meagher's horse was torn from under him by a rifled cannon ball, he jumped up, waved his sword, and exclaimed, 'Boys! look at the flag — remember Ireland and Fontenoy.'*

Advancing through blinding smoke and deafening gunfire, the regiment successfully pushed the enemy from the hill. After the position was in Federal hands, Major General Irvin McDowell, commander of the Union forces, personally thanked the Irishmen for their efforts and success.

But the day was not won. Fresh Confederate troops were brought up and forced the Federals from the hill, capturing hundreds of Union prisoners in the process. The green flag with the golden harp of Erin remained a desired symbol for the Confederates.

> *One of our wounded men who carried the flag was shot down, and the flag was torn from his grasp. Raising himself up, he again attacked his Rebel antagonist, struck him down, and carried off one of the Secession flags; but this was not long to remain with him, for he was again charged upon, and the trophy taken from him, besides being taken prisoner. However, having concealed a revolver, he shot down the two soldiers in charge of him, and captured a captain's sword and a prisoner, both of which he brought safety [sic] to our camp. His name is John Keefe, and he is worthy of being recorded among our truly brave men.*

Unable to hold their position, the Federal forces began to retire from the field. The retreat was bedlam, although the 69th retired in order:

> *Our Colonel, too, showed the greatest coolness and bravery throughout the fight. He stood to the last and rallied the remnant of his shattered forces, and took us off the field in a square and with our colors flying high; but he didn't do this till after all the other regiments had retired or were well retiring.*

The main thoroughfare back to Washington, the Warrenton Turnpike, was clogged with the wagons of spectators, artillery caissons, ambulances, and a flood of humanity fleeing the horrors of the battlefield. Captain D.P. Conyngham wrote of the retreat to Washington,

> *Artillery horses had their traces cut, and were mounted by officers, privates, and civilians, who made flank movements through the fields. There was a regular mingling and confusion of soldiers without arms, members of Congress and editors without hats or coats, ladies in buggies, wagons, and on horseback...*

As the Confederates pursued the fleeing Union troops, hundreds of Federal prisoners were captured. Captain Conyngham continued:

> *The Sixty-ninth left the Field in good order, with colors flying. Colonel Corcoran formed the remnant of his forces into a kind of square to meet the charge of cavalry, which they repulsed. As they gained the road they were again*

charged on, and Colonel Corcoran was wounded through the leg. The crowd and pressure of the fugitive troops rushing by was so great, and the confusion so general, that his men lost sight of him, and he fell into the enemy's hands...

Michael Cavanagh, author of General Meagher's memoirs, wrote of the regiment's arrival back in camp the following morning:

At 3 o'clock on the morning of the 22d of July, weary and worn, famished and naked almost, the 69th passed through the familiar gates of their old quarters, and after a battle which had lasted for eight hours and more and a march of five and thirty miles laid themselves down to sleep.

Although the men of the 69th had dem-onstrated their bravery, the cost was high. The regiment's casualties in the battle totalled 192 men, including 95 who were missing or captured.

Ironically, the men of the 69th New York State Militia would not have had to fight at Bull Run. Their term of service had already expired before the battle. In his **Memoirs of Chaplain Life**, Irish Brigade chaplain, Father William Corby, wrote:

The soldiers, at the President's call, had enlisted for ninety days only; and before the memorable battle of the First Bull Run, which took place July 21, 1861, the term having expired in the case of several regiments, on the 20th... The Sixty-ninth agreed to continue. They did so, and 'fought like Turks.' After this battle was over, the Sixty-ninth was disbanded in New York, the time having expired sometime before.

The "Prince of Wales" Flag

While visiting Canada in October, 1860 Queen Victoria's son, the Prince of Wales, was invited to visit the United States by President James Buchanan. Two events were planned to honor the Prince in New York City, a ball and a parade of the city's regiments.

Colonel Michael Corcoran, commander of the 69th New York State Militia, refused to allow his regiment to participate in a parade which honored, "a sovereign under whose reign Ireland was made a desert and her sons forced into exile." Corcoran was arrested and his action created a national uproar. Letters and telegrams of support were sent to Corcoran, as well as gifts; including a green Irish flag with the proclamation, "Presented to the 69th Regiment in commemoration of the 11th October 1860."

Before Corcoran could be tried, Fort Sumter was attacked and war became imminent. Corcoran was released and the 69th became part of the forces defending Washington, D.C. With the regiment went the "Prince of Wales" flag, which was carried proudly at the battle of Bull Run.

"Prince of Wales" Flag *Courtesy of Ken Powers*

"Oh, I remember well that dreary morning! It was not frosty, but a raw wind, and a miserable, drizzling rain chilled us as we were hastily prepared to depart on our first march—our first campaign. It took a long time to get everything ready."

—Father William Corby
Memoirs of Chaplain Life

ALONG THE PENINSULA AND IN THE SEVEN DAYS

It was during Major General George B. McClellan's Peninsula Campaign, in the spring and early summer of 1862, that General Meagher's Irish Brigade learned for the first time the privations of being a soldier.

Father William Corby recalled the soldier's introduction to marching:

The roads were in a terrible condition, and the poor men who loaded themselves before starting from camp, with boots, stockings, underwear, etc., kept casting them off on the roadside as they felt themselves unable to carry them any longer.

Corby also recalled a halt made by the brigade near Fair Oaks after a day of hard marching:

We halted in the dark on a field nearly surrounded by woods, and tried to rest for a short time on the wet ground, to recover some of the strength lost by the fatigues of the night. In the morning when we opened our eyes we found that we had been sleeping with the dead! Many a poor soldier lay cold in death just where he fell in the battle the previous evening, and we saw the ghastly appearance of their bodies,

which had been, as it were, our bedfellows, and a shudder passed through our heart.

By the battle of Malvern Hill, July 1, 1862, the brigade had already developed a reputation as hard, dependable fighters. Captain D.P. Conyngham wrote:

Stragglers, wounded, and retreating lines cheer on the Irish Brigade, as it proudly and defiantly dashes forward. They gain the hill top amidst showers of shot and shell, and defiantly reply to it with a continual musketry fire. As they advanced they met remnants of the brave Ninth Massachusetts, bearing their dying colonel to the rear, who greeted them with hearty cheers...
The cannon and musketry of the enemy were sweeping this hill. It was one sheet of molten lead, roundshot and shell ricocheting over it.

Conyngham wrote of the later stages of the fight:

The Eighty-eighth in a moment dashes in with the Sixty-ninth, under a fierce fire from the enemy, who are concealed in the woods and a neighbor-

ing house; still, there is no faltering, but wild cheers, and on they press for the hill-top, where a hand-to-hand fight ensues. Men brain and bayonet each other. The enemy makes a bold stand to hold the hill, but in vain. They sullenly retire, but the darkness prevents our brave fellows from following them up. They send a parting good-night after them. Malvern Hill is fought. McClellan's army is saved, but that hillside is covered with the dying and the dead of the Irish Brigade.

The spirit of the men of the Irish Brigade is demonstrated in the following story, related by Irish Brigade historian Conyngham:

Lieutenant John H. Donovan, of Company D, Sixty-ninth Regiment, afterwards captain, while in the act of charging with his company, was shot through the ear just under the brain, and was left for dead. Next morning Generals Hill and Magruder went round to the several officers and demanded their side-arms and revolvers. On coming to young Donovan, Hill demanded his. Donovan replied that he had sent them to his regiment by his servant after falling. 'I think,' said the general,' from the apparent nature of your wound, you won't have much need of them in the future.'

'I think differently, general,' replied the other, indignantly: 'I think I have one good eye left yet, and will risk that in the cause of the Union. Should I

National color carried by the 69th New York Infantry. *Courtesy of Ken Powers.*

ever lose that, I shall go it blind!'

'What command do you belong to?'

'Meagher's Irish Brigade.'

'Oh, indeed!' said the other, passing on.

Donovan survived his wound and capture by the Confederates. In his history of the Irish Brigade, Conyngham quoted a letter written to General Meagher by Donovan from Bellevue Hospital in New York City:

I was told in Richmond [after being captured], that had they known the precise whereabouts of the Irish Brigade on the field, they would have sent a whole division to take itself and General Meagher prisoners, and hang the 'exiled traitor' from the highest tree in Richmond. I told them they would need several divisions to accomplish that job, and that even then they couldn't do it.

Father William Corby recalled the Federal withdrawl following the battle of Malvern Hill:

As we retired, in our well-ordered retreat, toward our new position on the James River, we were obliged to abandon all our wounded who were not able to walk or to get transportation. All the ambulances were very soon full. Wounded men crawled on to army wagons; others hobbled along, their wounds still undressed, and from loss of blood becoming all the while weaker and fainter. Many held on till their last breath, to avoid capture and to be with their companions. From the wounded in the ambulances, from those clinging on to the rear ends of the army wagons, and from those limping along on foot,

blood was dripping all along the road, and thus the blood of heroes marked our way as the march continues to a position more suitable for a systematic and obstinate contest.

The Peninsula campaign and the battles of the Seven Days had tested the mettle of the men of the Irish Brigade. Along the muddy roads and on the smoke filled battlefields they had passed from starry-eyed recruits to battle hardened veterans. They had truly seen "the elephant."

The next great test for the men of the Irish Brigade would come in a cornfield owned by a farmer named Roulette, near a creek called Antietam.

Members of the Irish Brigade at Harrison's Landing in the early summer of 1862. Father William Corby sits in the lower right corner. *Mass. MOLLUS Collection, USAMHI.*

"All his campaigning is his courtship, and the day of battle is his bridal day, when he is wedded to his mistress — Death."

—"Antietam—The Dead of the Brigade"
quoted from a New York newspaper

BLOODY WEDNESDAY:
THE BATTLE OF ANTIETAM

After the hard fought battles of South Mountain, Major General George B. McClellan's Army of the Potomac followed Robert E. Lee's Army of Northern Virginia through the southern Maryland countryside to the tiny village of Sharpsburg; where Lee spread the wings of his army along the banks of Antietam Creek.

In a brief history of the 69th New York, Colonel James J. Smith recalled the regiment's crossing of the creek on September 16:

We forded the creek, by General Meagher's orders, taking off our shoes (those who could, many were barefoot, and some, like the writer, were so foot-sore that they had not been able to take off their shoes or what remained of them, for a week), to wring out their socks, so as to not incumber the men in active movements, and every man was required to fill his canteen.

The next morning, an unknown officer of the 63rd New York wrote a letter describing the night before the battle:

The night was not as inclement as I had anticipated, and we derived 'aid and comfort' from a stack of straw which lay 'appropriately' in our vicinity. About 2 a.m., we heard our pickets exchange volleys with those of enemy;

but, after a time, all was quiet again. About 4 we commenced preparing our breakfast; but had not time to eat it, when our line of batteries opened on the Rebels, who promptly replied, and the cannonading is now, at this hour, (7 o'clock) without intermission.

The unknown officer also wrote of the Confederate bombardment:

The Rebels must have been very short of missiles, when they fire off old sledges, horse-shoes, old iron; and in one instance a mule of ours was struck with the leg of a cooking stove! They must have also been short of shells—otherwise, they would not have fired so many solid shot.

Colonel Smith recalled General Meagher's dress for the impending battle:

On Wednesday, September 17, 1862, General Meagher, gotten up most gorgeously in a somewhat fancy uniform, with a gold shoulder-belt, was carefully brushed by an orderly, and remarked that 'we'd all have a brush soon.' We had it.

The battle shifted along the Confederate line to a well defended position in a sunken road hidden below the brow of the hill. It was against this sunken road, soon to gain the sobriquet "bloody lane," that the Irish Brigade was sent.

In an article for the **Philadelphia Hibernian**, Brevet Major General St. Clair A. Mulholland, of the 116th Pennsylvania, described the opening stages of the assault:

> *As they went on the double-quick over the cornstalks, crash came a volley on the right of the line, and the Twenty-ninth [Massachusetts] got a*

Thomas Francis Meager in a Patriotic pose. *Mass. MOLLUS Collection, USAMHI*

> *dose. The Sixty-third caught it; the Eighty-eighth coming up in time to get its share of the first course of the heavy repast that was to ensue. This was followed by a brief rest in the deep fur-*

rows of the field with the sharpshooters busy picking off great numbers of our men.

An unknown participant of the battle also recorded the initial stages of the attack:

> *All this time the bullets are whirring about, an occasional wounded man falls down and is borne to the rear; — but we have not yet commenced to fire. Suddenly, as if planted there in defiance, the flags of the rebel regiments, on the rising ground, are waving within easy distance—ours floats as proudly, as steadily in line.*

The writer continued:

> *Moving along, the shot and shell of the enemy poured over our heads, and crashed in the hollows in the rear, or among the occasional trees behind; on the right, the sound of musketry was deafening, and the Brigade soon came within range of the enemy's small arms. The advance, however, was uninterrupted, unbroken, although it had to be made under many difficulties, the chief of which was the close, compact, and strong fences, which impeded the progress of the men, and the crossing of which, of course, caused a momentary derangement of the dressing.*

Brigade historian Conyngham wrote:

> *The fight here was terrific. The rebels were entrenched and screened in the sunken road, all the time pouring a deadly fire into the advancing column of the Brigade. The green flag was completely riddled, and it appeared certain death to any one to bear it, for eight*

color-bearers had already fallen. The last had fallen, and the Irish green lay trailing in the dust. Meagher called out—'Boys, raise the colors, and follow me!'

Captain James McGee, of the Sixty-ninth, rushed forward, and crying, 'I'll follow you!' seized the flag.

As he raised it, a bullet cut the standard in two in his hand; and, as he again stooped down, another bullet tore through his cap. Still, he jumped up, waved the flag, shook it at the rebels, and cheered on the troops, almost miraculously escaping.

Conyngham also described a close brush with death experienced by Thomas Francis Meagher:

General Meagher's clothes were perforated with bullets; his horse was shot under him, and being stunned by the fall, had to be carried to the rear; while Lieutenant [James E.] Mackey, of his staff, received his death-wound when carrying out an order of the general's.

A New York newspaper described one of the best documented incidents of the battle, the death of Captain Patrick Clooney, of the 88th New York:

Struck in the knee, and severely wounded unto lameness, besought by everyone to go to the rear and be attended to, he peremptorily refuses to go. He seizes the colors, when the color-bearer was shot down, and in this position, limping on one foot, his voice still ringing, hopeful, resonant, he is struck by two bullets—and falls down stiff, and stark and cold, the lifeless hand hold-

ing, with the grip of fate, the Green Banner which in life he loved so well.

In his history of the Irish Brigade, Conyngham quotes Captain Edward Field regarding the fate of the Irish flag carried by the 63rd New York:

The rebels seemed to have a special spite against the green flag, and five color-bearers were shot down successively in a short time. As the last man fell even these Irishmen hesitated a moment to assume a task synonymous with death. 'Big [John] Gleason,' Captain of the Sixty-third, six feet seven, sprang forward and snatched it up. In a few minutes a bullet struck the staff, shattering it to pieces; Gleason tore the flag from the broken staff, wrapped it around his body, putting his sword-belt over it, and went through the rest of that fight untouched.

Colonel Smith wrote of the 69th New York:

The Bloody Lane was the witness of the efficacy of the buck-and-ball at close quarters. We carried the way and the way beyond, leaving on the ground a lot of flags which we were too busy to pick up, for the capture of which Medals of Honor were freely bestowed on the men of another regiment, whose commander was an able performer on the trumpet of self-laudation.

In a letter to a New York newspaper, Captain Michael O'Sullivan, Company F, 63rd New York, described the heavy casualties suffered by his regiment:

We have fought the enemy, and our

brigade has been cut to pieces! Every man in my company has either been killed or wounded, with the exception of eleven. I received a rifle shot through the left thigh, going completely through—fortunately without touching

Federal forces were able to push the Confederates from the Sunken Road and the exhausted survivors of the attack were forced to tend to the wounded. Father William Corby wrote:

All the wounded of our brigade,

Weapons and accouterment types of the Irish Brigade. Top, Model 1861 Rifle Musket, Caliber .58 carried by the 116th Pennsylvania. Bottom, smoothbore Model 1842 musket, caliber .69 carried by the New York regiments. The 28th Massachusetts was armed with the Model 1853 Enfield Rifle Musket. (Not shown)
CWLM.

the bone. Poor Lieut. Henry McConnell was shot through the brain, and never spoke again. P.W. Lyndon, my First Lieutenant, was shot through the heart.... All the line officers of our regiment are either killed or wounded, save one Captain and five Lieutenants.

After nearly three hours of fighting, the

numbering hundreds, were carried to a large straw-stack, which had to answer for a hospital. Here they had dry straw at least; but during the day, as they could not get into the shadow of the stack, the hot sun made it very uncomfortable for them. Here I saw one poor man with a bullet in his forehead, and his brains protruding from the hole made by the ball. Strange to say, he lived three days, but was speechless, and deaf, and had lost his senses entirely.

Once again, the men of the Irish Brigade had paid a heavy price to demonstrate their bravery. Brigade historian Conyngham described the scene of the battle that evening:

The troops lay beside their stacked arms in the battle-field all night. The mournful cry of the whippoor-will, and the croaking of the frogs in the marshes, mingled with the groans of the dying and wounded, broke the solemn stillness that reigned over the field of carnage.

The chaplains were quietly moving over the field with lamps in their hands, shriving the penitent, and binding up the wounds of the suffering. The doctors too, were moving among the groups of the dead and wounded, stanching their wounds, or easing their sufferings.

"To charge an enemy or enter a battle when one knows that there is no hope of success, requires courage of a much higher order than when the soldier is sustained by the enthusiasm born of hope."

—*St. Clair A. Mulholland*

FREDERICKSBURG

Having replaced George B. McClellan as commander of the Army of the Potomac, Major General Ambrose Burnside led his army to Stafford Heights along the banks of the Rappahannock River, overlooking the city of Fredericksburg, Virginia. For nearly a month Burnside watched Robert E. Lee strengthen his defenses, anchored on the heights surrounding the town. Finally, Burnside decided to attack Lee on December 13. As part of Major General Edwin V. Sumner's Right Grand Division, the Irish Brigade was given the task of attacking the Confederate defenses at Marye's Heights and a low stone wall and sunken road which ran below the heights.

As the troops moved down Stafford Heights to cross the river they were met by enterprising embalmers. St. Clair Mulholland recalled years later:

Not so pleasant was the reception of the professional embalmers who, alive to business, thrust their cards into the hands of the men as they went along, said cards being suggestive of an early trip home, nicely boxed up and delivered to loving friends by express, sweet as a nut and in perfect preservation, etc., etc.

Second Army Corps historian Francis A. Walker recalled a scene of plundering within Fredericksburg the day before the battle:

Thus the writer recollects seeing one gigantic private of the Irish Brigade wearing the white satin bonnet of some fair 'Secesh' bride; while another sported a huge 'scoop' bonnet of the olden time. A coffee pot that would hold ten gallons, and which had evidently done duty at church festivals, was the plunder of a third member of this rollicking band; another was staggering under a monstrous feather-bed for two...

In his history of the 116th Pennsylvania Infantry, Mulholland recalled the night before the battle:

The night of the 12th was to the men of the Regiment one of the most dismal and miserable ever experienced. The cold was bitter and penetrating. The troops massed so close that there was not even enough room for the men to lie down on the ground, and it was a fortunate man who could secure a cracker box to sit upon during the weary hours. Sleep was impossible, it was so cold and chilly. Groups of officers occupied the parlors of the fashionable residences, spending the night in song and story; and Southern pianos played accompaniments to 'Hail Columbia' and the 'Star Spangled Banner.'

Colonel James J. Smith recalled, "The night was remarkable for a wonderfully brilliant aurora borealis, which was supplemented by the flames of the burning town and the glowing trains of bursting shells."

In an unpublished letter written to Francis A. Walker in 1883, W.G. Mitchell, of Major General Winfield Scott Hancock's staff, recalled an incident immediately before the Brigade made the assault against the Confederate position at Marye's Heights:

You doubtless remember when we assaulted 'Marye's' Heights, ('Fredericksburg') Dec. 13, 1862[,] the soldiers of the Irish Brigade placed little sprigs of 'green' in their caps just before the order was given to advance to the attack. The Brigade had stacked arms in the street. A house near by was over grown with an ever green vine, box I believe, and each man of the Irish Brigade passed over it and pulling off a bit of the green stuck it in the front of his cap. In a few moments afterwards the word was given for the assault and very soon a number of the gallant fellows lay dead and wounded with the little green sprigs on their heads.

At the same time, small wreaths of boxwood were made and placed around the finials of the battle-worn Brigade flags.

In another previously unpublished letter, written in 1881, Robert Nugent, commander of the 69th New York, described the opening of the assault made by the Irish Brigade:

When the Brigade received the order in Fredericksburgh [sic] to proceed to the front the 69th led the advance through the City and across the

Mill Race which ran parallel to the City, to the rising ground a short distance from the Mill Race on the right followed by the 88th New York when they halted. The 116th Penn, the 28th Mass, and the 63rd New York received orders to form on the left by the command 'On the right by file into line[.]' After the formation

Colonel Robert Nugent, 69th New York Infantry. Note "69" in the laurel wreath on Nugent's hat and the use use of the officer's hat cord as a string tie.
Roger Hunt Collection, USAMHI.

of the Brigade as above, it made its celebrated charge on the renowned stone wall.

Before the Brigade was sent forward, two companies of the 69th New York were sent to the right to guard against an attack by the enemy from that direction.

Mulholland recalled the opening of the attack:

As they moved out Hanover Street, the city seeming so deserted, and in a manner quiet, the men spoke in low whispers and solitary tones. A lone, solitary pussy cat sat on a gate-post mewing dolefully.

In his history of the 116th Pennsylvania, Mulholland wrote:

Just before moving from this spot one of the young officers of the Regiment, a brave boy from Chester Country, Pennsylvania, Lieutenant Seneca G. Willauer, was badly torn by a shell which stripped the flesh from his thigh and left the bone, for four or five inches, white and bare. He approached the regimental commander and, holding the bleeding limb for inspection, said, with the most gentle manner and placid voice, 'Colonel, do you think that I should go on with my company or go to the hospital?' No doubt had he been told to go with his company he would have done so.

In an article written for the **Philadelphia Weekly Times** series "Annals of the War," Mulholland described the effectiveness of the Confederate artillery fire:

Shells began dropping with destructive effect. One striking the Eighty-eighth New York placed eighteen men hors du combat. I will ever remember the first one that burst in my regiment—wounding the colonel, cutting off the head of Sergeant Marley and killing two or three others. I was struck by the instantaneousness of the deaths. The column had halted for a moment, a sharp report, a puff of smoke and three or four men lay stark dead, their faces calm, their eyes mild and life-like, lips unmoved, no sigh of pain and suffering. Marley had not fallen, but dropped upon his knees, his musket clasped in both hands and resting upon the ground.

In the same article, Mulholland wrote, "The wounded went past in great numbers, and the appearance of the dripping blood was not calculated to enthuse the men or cheer them for the first important battle."

In his history of the Second Army Corps, Francis A. Walker recounted the initial stages of the assault made by the brigade:

Right gallantly the Irishmen charge over the sheltering ridge, and dash across the bloody spaces strewn with the dead and dying of the brigades that have gone on before....

Walker continued:

The killed and wounded fall like leaves in the autumn, while hundreds of men, brave among the bravest, lie down beneath the storm of lead. [Colonel Robert] Nugent and [Colonel Patrick] Kelly, to whom the Irish Brigade has become accustomed to look for examples of courage and devotion, are at the front; with their own hands they under-

take to tear down fences and make a way to the stone wall.

In a short historical sketch on the 63rd New York, Major John Dwyer wrote of the heavy fire into which the Brigade advanced:

Canister shot, shrapnel, and shell ploughed the ground all round this devoted brigade, but they faltered not; they

Colonel Patrick Kelly, killed in action near Petersburg on 16 June 1864. *Mass. MOLLUS Collection, USAMHI*

rushed on to their doom. Arriving a few rods from the famous stone wall sheets of flame from thousands of muskets, withheld until this moment, assaulted them. Men fell in groups along the en-

tire front of those five regiments, until nothing remained but skeletons of companies.

As with all battles, the color-bearers became prominent targets for the enemy, and every regiment would afterward tell stories of the men who carried their flags. Major John Dwyer, of the 63rd New York, wrote, "The colors of the Sixty-third were torn into shreds and a canister shot shattered the staff. Color Sergeant Chambers (an Albany man) had his coat honey-combed with bullets and grape-shot, but he miraculously escaped."

The color sergeant of the 69th New York was not so fortunate. In his history of the Brigade, Conyngham wrote:

The flag of the Sixty-ninth was lost during the fight, and the men felt very uneasy about it, for it was their proud boast that they never lost a flag.

Next day the color-sergeant was discovered sitting up against a tree, dead, and his hands clasped on his breast, as if protecting something. Near him was the staff of the missing flag. When removing the body, the men found the flag wrapped around it, with a bullet hole right through it and his heart.

St. Clair Mulholland also recalled an incident concerning the colors of the 116th Pennsylvania's flag:

The color sergeant, William H. Tyrell, went down on one knee (his other leg being shattered) still waving the flag on the crest. Five balls struck him in succession; a dozen pierced the colors; and another broke the flag-staff, and the colors and the color sergeant fell together. The orders to retire passed down the line and the command began fall-

ing back. All the color guard was down, and the flag in the grasp of young Tyrell was still on the fire swept crest. It was soon missed, and that fearless soldier, Lieutenant Francis T. Quinlan, ran back to save it. A hundred fired at him, but quickly seizing the broken flag-staff he threw himself on the ground and, with the flag tightly clasped to his breast, rolled back to where the command had halted, a noble deed, well done.

As with the units which preceded them against Marye's Heights, the Irish Brigade could not withstand the overwhelming fire from the enemy, and their attack was broken. Francis A. Walker wrote:

Flesh and blood will not stand it any longer. In the face of the manifest impossibility of accomplishing anything, a part of the brigade take to the ground; a part break to the rear, are reformed by Meagher, who, in his strange, unaccountable way, has been separated from his command during its charge—and at last find their way to the city, and even across the river.

Mulholland described the scene of the battlefield after the attack had failed:

It was a long, dreadful afternoon that awaited the thousands of wounded, who lay scattered over the sad and ghastly plain. The only place of cover was the brick house out near the stone wall. To this, hundreds of the wounded dragged themselves and a great mass of sufferers huddled together and struggled to get nearer the house that they might escape the fire. All around the great heaps of dead bore testimony to the fierceness of combat. Near by, a

color sergeant lay, stark and cold, with the flag of his regiment covering him. Just in front of the stone wall lay a line of men of the Irish Brigade, with the green box-wood in their caps, and the two bodies nearest the enemy were those of Major William Horgan and Adjutant John R. Young, both of the Eighty-eighth New York.

One survivor recalled the night the brigade spent on the battlefield:

A cold, bitter, bleak December night closed upon that field of blood and carnage. Thousands lay along that hillside, and in the valleys, whose oozing wounds were frozen, and whose cold limbs were stiffened, for they had no blankets; they had flung them away going into the fight. Masses of the dead and dying were huddled together; some convulsed in the last throes of death; others gasping for water—delirious, writhing in agony, and stiffened with the cold frost. The living tried to shelter themselves behind the dead.

All that remained was for the surgeons to do their grizzly duty. In an article written for the **Philadelphia Weekly Times** series "Annals of the War," Mulholland recalled the scene in one of the hospitals:

The cases here are all capital and amputation is nearly always resorted to. Hands and feet, arms and legs are thrown under each table and the sickening piles grow large as the night progresses. The delicate limbs of the drummer boy fall along with the rough hand of the veteran in years, but all, every one is so brave and cheerful.

At sunrise, Sunday morning, May 3, 1863, the battle opened with terrific cannonading. Simultaneously commenced the bursting of shells and the harsh, crashing sound of musketry, reminding one of a dreadful storm, the coming of mighty, angry winds, driving the dark and threatening clouds, sweeping everything material in their path, the rolling reverberations of great thunder-bolts that seem to give fitting expressions to the thoughts of an offended God.

— Father William Corby
Memoirs of Chaplain Life

CHANCELLORSVILLE

After command of the Army of the Potomac passed from Major General Ambrose Burnside to Major General Joseph Hooker, the Federal army crossed the Rappahannock River in late April, 1863, and began to move against the Army of Northern Virginia. With only half of his army present, Robert E. Lee made a series of bold moves, including splitting his army in the face of the enemy, and met the advancing foe near the crossroads village of Chancellorsville. What followed has often been called Lee's greatest battle.

In a post-war newspaper article, one participant recalled:

Sunday, May 3, broke forth bright and clear. The birds in the forest were chanting sweet melody: but their music was soon interrupted by the fierce roll of artillery. About five o'clock in the morning the battle was resumed, the batteries in our front vomiting forth their horrid missiles of death. Indeed, the battle opened so fiercely that the booming of artillery shook the earth around as if convulsed by an earthquake.

St. Clair Mulholland recorded a scene as the Irish Brigade marched toward Chancellorsville on the morning of May 3:

During a moment's halt, with the
shells falling and exploding around him, Sergeant Bernard McCahey looking back, waved his hand to the earth and air and in the most ludicrous manner exclaimed, 'Good boi wurreld.' Another son of Erin said to his companion, 'What are we going in here for, Jimmy?' 'To be after making history, Barney, to be sure.'

Mulholland also recalled fleeing wounded soldiers as the Brigade marched toward the battle:

Streams of wounded men flowed to the rear. Men with torn faces, split heads, smashed arms, wounded men assisting their more badly hurt comrades, stretchers bearing to the rear men whose limbs were crushed and mangled, and others who had no limbs at all. Four soldiers carried on two muskets, which they held in form of a litter, the body of their Lieutenant-Colonel who had just been killed. The body hung over the muskets, the head and feet limp and dangling, the blood dripping from a ghastly wound — a terrible sight indeed.

The Brigade was deployed near the Chancellor House, for which the crossroads was named, in support of the 5th Maine Artillery.

Mulholland noted the calm the men of the 116th Pennsylvania exhibited under heavy artillery fire:

> *Captain [Garrett] Nowlen sat in the road, humming a tune, filled his pipe, lit it with the burning fuse of a Confederate shell, and began smoking. Corporal Emsley, of the color guard, was passing jokes with Abe Detwiler, the color sergeant; and one would suppose that the boys were listening to church bells, on that sweet Sunday morning, instead of the rush and scream of the shells.*

In a post-war article, an unknown participant described General Thomas Francis Meagher:

> *With Meagher at its head the brigade marched as cooly and steadily as if on parade. As we marched through the woods shot and shell were poured like hail upon us. When the General reached the end of the road he turned the head of the column and deployed into the woods. His escapes were almost miraculous; for, though the men were falling on every side, he boldly rode on, all the time cheering the men by word and example. Here a shell burst behind him, where he had just left, killing four or five men.*

In another newspaper article, an unknown participant wrote:

> *The brigade remained in the woods for about two hours, under a most destructive fire of shot and shell, which killed two officers and several men. The Fifth Maine battery was placed at the opening of the wood, commanding the plain towards Chancellorsville. This battery was well worked and did good execution; for not until all the men and horses were killed or wounded did it cease firing.*

In an article for the **Watertown (New York) Daily Times** about a tour of the Fredericksburg and Chancellorsville battlefields in 1899, Albert D. Shaw wrote:

> *Another orderly fell from his horse with his bowels protruding. Many of the regiments were wounded. Duffy, of Company A [116th Pennsylvania], was lying with a piece of his skull crushed in. Dan Rogers, a boy, had his shoulder blade smashed; but the men kept wonderfully calm.*

Soon the Chancellor House became a victim of the heavy artillery bombardment. Mulholland wrote:

> *From the dense volumes of smoke that arose from the Chancellorsville house and the forest in our front it was evident that they were on fire. This was the more melancholy, as the house was used as a hospital, and the wood was full of our dead and wounded. So thick was the smoke from the burning forest and the continual firing that the plain was obscured. Indeed it was said to reflect that our brave wounded companions were left to perish the most horrible of deaths. Yet such are the casualties of war.*

Father William Corby also recalled the fate of another wounded soldier:

> *While in the woods the surgeons had a man on a rude table that had been*

constructed from planks found at Chancellorsville, and while they were getting ready to amputate a limb, a cannon-ball swept the man off the table, smashing him to pieces, and left the terrified surgeons on either side of the table almost paralyzed with consternation.

As the Union line disintegrated, little remained in the area except for the Irish Brigade

St. Clair A. Mulholland as a Brevet Brigadier General. *Mass. MOLLUS Collection, USAMHI*

and the 5th Maine battery. In a post-war newspaper article, Mulholland recalled:

Soon nothing was left near the Chancellorsville house except the Irish Brigade and the almost silenced battery. One gun was still firing, however, and

a gallant corporal and one man still clung to the piece and fired it when all others had gone. It was time for the last troops to fall back, and the order came to the 116th Pennsylvania volunteers to save the abandons guns. One hundred of the men were soon detailed to rush forward and surround the pieces and drag them to the rear, which was done in splendid style. As the squad was tugging away at one of the guns, trying to get it started, a shell burst in their midst, killing Theodore Walker and George Rushworth, of Co. D, wounding half a dozen others and knocking everyone over on their backs. The men jumped to their feet and rushed at it again laughing at the mishap, and pulled it off.

Irish Brigade historian D.P. Conyngham recalled the recovery of the guns:

As we dragged out the batter, the cheering and excitement were unbounded, and the rebel batteries continued raining shot and shell around us. Here Captain Lynch was killed, being cut right through the centre with a solid shot.

Mulholland also recalled the death of John C. Lynch, of the 63rd New York:

As the writer passed to the right he bade his friend, Major Lynch [sic], 'Good morning.' A moment afterwards Lynch fell dead, a shell driving his sword through his body, killing him instantly, and the handsome, noble fellow who had walked up the road so full of life and happiness, lay by the wayside, an unrecognizable mass of quivering flesh and bones.

"Fan," the pet dog of Captain J.W. Byron, of the 88th New York, demonstrated her bravery in the battle. Conyngham noted:

Fan went into every battle, and while the firing was brisk lay down behind a big log or in some other secure place; and when a lull would follow she'd sally out, and run along the regiment to see if any of her friends were killed or hurt.

She was very much attached to a man of the company, who during the firing fell mortally wounded. When Fan came up to him, she threw herself on him and cried, she wept and licked him, while the poor fellow would throw out his hand to pat her as he feebly exclaimed, 'Poor Fan! Poor Fan!'

The day after the battle, Colonel Richard C. Bentley, of the 63rd New York, wrote to his father:

We have had a terrible battle, lasting since Thursday. I went in yesterday, commanding the balance of my regiment and the 69th put together, about 160 men. We did not get under musketry fire, but the shelling was terrible. As I marched along the road to get in position, a shell struck the centre of my line and killed one and wounded two men of the 69th. I received a piece of shell, burst in the air, on the head, which passed through the centre of the top of my hat, grazing my head, without cutting out the side, through the rim, and tore through my coat, vest and shirt, at the back of my left shoulder. I remained in command nearly an hour before I felt any effect, save a slight shock. The sun was very hot, and after getting them into the last position they occupied before being withdrawn, I sat down and keeled over and was taken to the rear.

A year later, the survivors of the Irish Brigade occupied the same ground during the Wilderness Campaign. Lieutenant Colonel Richard C. Dale, of the 116th Pennsylvania, wrote to a Pittsburgh newspaper:

By the way, the battlefield is covered with wild flowers, nearly all of a purple color as though the blood of our brave soldiers had so drenched the soil as to darken the very flowers that grew upon it. Perhaps some who have lost friends at Chancellorsville may take pleasure in thinking that though their dead heroes may sleep in unmarked graves, yet the flowers grow over them as profusely as if interred in any of our beautiful cemeteries at home.

Soon the lines were but a few feet apart, and the men returned the fire with deadly effect. Captain Nowlen drew his revolver and opened fire; nearly all the other officers followed his example. Little Jeff Carl killed a man within six feet of his bayonet. That hero, Sergeant Francis Malin, was conspicuous by his dash and bravery, as his tall form towered above all around him — a noble soul. He soon fell dead with a bullet in his brain.

— *St. Clair A. Mulholland*

"An Alley of Death"
GETTYSBURG

Early on the morning of June 28, 1863, Major General George Gordon Meade was awakened by a courier and informed that he had been given command of the Army of the Potomac, replacing Major General Joseph Hooker.

The Federal army had been pursuing the Army of Northern Virginia since early June. Father William Corby recounted the sights and sounds of the army as it marched at night:

Late in the evening the march of a tired army is a sight. As a rule, not a voice is heard. Fatigue and drowsiness, added to a rather weak and fainting feeling, indispose men to converse, and by silent consent each one discontinues conversation. The click of a large spur, the occasional rattle of a sword, and other mechanical movements are the only sounds heard above the slow, steady tramp of the line and the heavy tread of the few horses that carry the mounted officers.

The two great armies met near the tiny crossroads town of Gettysburg, Pennsylvania on the morning of July 1. What ensued has come to be the most famous battle of the Civil War.

The men of the Irish Brigade arrived at Gettysburg on the early morning of July 2, and were held in reserve.

Late that afternoon, they were sent in to support Major General Daniel Sickles' crumbling line which ran through the Wheatfield, in an area now known as "The Loop". Because of heavy losses, only the 28th Massachusetts fought as a regiment; the 63rd, 69th, 88th New York, and the 116th Pennsylvania were represented by two companies each.

Before the Brigade went into action, Father William Corby stood on a low rock and gave the men absolution. Years later, at the dedication of Irish Brigade monuments at Gettysburg, Denis Burke recalled:

The brigade were kneeling and our faithful Chaplain, Father Corby, invoked the Divine blessing on their cause and undertaking. Rising from that posture, the command 'Forward!' is heard along the line; and fortified with religious consolation the Irish Brigade advanced, carrying the Stars and Stripes and the old Green Flag of Erin — the two flags they had already followed through so many battlefields. On and through the wheat that covered the ground, they advanced gradually and surely, losing many of their number, until out of the 530 who advanced, 195 are killed and wounded before they are brought to a halt.

Father William Corby, chaplain of the 88th New York Infantry, giving absolution to the men of the Irish Brigade before they enter the maelstrom of "the Wheatfield" at Gettysburg on 2 July 1863. *Mass. MOLLUS Collection, USAMHI.*

Today's visitor to Gettysburg will find a statue of Father William Corby standing on the same rock where he performed the absolution more than a century and a quarter ago.

In an article written for the **Philadelphia Times** series "Annals of the War," St. Clair A. Mulholland wrote:

> We had hardly got under way when the enemy's batteries opened and shells began falling all around us. The ground on which this division faced the enemy the afternoon of the 2d had already been fought over again and again, and the field and woods were strewn with killed or wounded.

In his history of the Irish Brigade, D.P.

Conyngham also recalled the artillery:

> About half-past four p.m., our line, which had commenced an advance, was met by a terrific cannonade, opened on its center and left, from the rebel batteries, masked with woods and grain fields. Our rifled-guns replied with effect, and for two hours the air seemed literally filled with screaming messengers of death.

The men of the Irish Brigade pushed through the Wheatfield to meet the advancing Confederates. Mulholland recalled for his "Annals of the War" article:

> As we approached the crest of the

**Monument at Gettysburg honoring Father Corby.
It is believed that the statue rests upon the same
rock on which Corby stood while giving absulution.**
Photo by Greg Thorpe

*fire, and for ten or fifteen minutes the
work of death went on. There was no
cheering, no time lost in unnecessary
movement. Every man there, both
Union and rebel, were veterans, and
knew just what was wanted. They stood
there face to face, loading and firing,
and so close that every shot told.*

As Mulholland recalled in the article, the
fire between the advancing Union and Confederate troops was tremendous and the terrain of
the area played a great role in the fight:

*They fired down while our men
fired upward, and our fire was more effective. On their line we found many
dead but few wounded —they were
nearly all hit in the head or the upper
part of the body. Behind one rock I
counted five dead bodies. This was some
of the most severe fighting our division
had ever done, and was so close that
the officers used their revolvers.*

Within a few minutes, the fighting became
so intense that in places it became hand-to-hand.
Mulholland then described a unique experience:

*In an instant our men and their
opponents were mingled together. In
charging we had literally ran right in
among them. Firing instantly ceased
and we found there was as many of the
enemy as there were of ourselves. Officers and men looked for a time utterly
bewildered; all the fighting had
stopped, yet the Graybacks still retained
their arms and had showed no disposition to surrender. At this moment a
Union Officer called out in a loud voice:
'The Confederate troops will lay down
there arms and go to the rear!' This
ended a scene that was becoming em-*

*rugged hill, from behind the huge boulders that were everywhere scattered
around, the men of Longstreet's corps
rose up and poured into our ranks a
most destructive fire. The sudden meeting astonished us, the lines being not
more than thirty feet apart when the firing opened. I cannot imagine why the
rebs allowed us to get so near before
firing, unless they thought we would
give way under the weight and impulse
of the attack.*

Mulholland continued:

Our men promptly returned the

barrassing. The Confederates promptly obeyed, and a large number of what I think were some of Kershaw's brigade became our prisoners.

But the Federal troops were sustaining great casualties and could not withstand the Confederate assault. Lines became mixed and survivors would later describe the Wheatfield as a whirlpool, sucking troops into it without any organization:

> *Some of the wounded who fell in the wheat field during the retreat of this division, and were forced to lie there between the two fires, fared badly. One man of my regiment fell shot through the leg, and while he lay there was hit five or six times. When it became evident that we had to fall back, our wounded, with visions of Andersonville and Libby before them, begged piteously to be taken along — many of them keeping with us, wholly unaided. Sergeant Thomas Grey was shot through the stomach and, with entrails protruding, managed to drag himself along and succeeded in escaping with us.*

After being trapped by the Confederates in the front and rear, the Federals in the Wheatfield broke for the safety of Little Round Top. Mulholland recalled, "Passing through this alley of death, where the bullets came thick as hail, we got away with a large part of the division, but the loss was terrible. In the half hour that we were there fourteen hundred men were lost."

Although their loss was great, that evening the Irish Brigade was moved to another position on Cemetery Ridge in preparation of another possible attack by Robert E. Lee. Mulholland described the night of July 2:

> *Few of us slept during the night.*

Our division went back and was put in position on Cemetery Ridge by General Hancock, who all the night long labored to strengthen this line. The men gathered rocks and fence rails and used them to erect a light breastwork. Had the necessary tools been distributed to the troops we could have entrenched this line and made it formidable, but we could not find a pick or a shovel, and the works that we did attempt were very light, scarcely sufficient to stop a musket ball. During the whole night mounted officers galloped to and fro, and troops were hurried to important points.

July 3 dawned hot and muggy. Along the Union line tired men waited for the expected activity from the Confederates. Mulholland continued:

> *About noon we could see considerable activity along Seminary Ridge. Battery after battery appeared along the edge of the woods. Guns were unlimbered, placed in position and the horses taken to the rear. On our side, officers sat around in groups and, through field glasses, anxiously watched these movements in our front and wondered what it all meant. Shortly after 1 o'clock, however, we knew all about it.*

Shortly after 1 p.m., two guns from the Washington Artillery fired signal shots opening one of the largest artillery bombardments ever to take place on the North American continent. In his article for the "Annals of the War" series, Mulholland wrote:

> *I have read many accounts of this artillery duel, but the most graphic description by the most able writers falls*

far short of the reality. No tongue or pen can find language strong enough to convey any idea of its awfulness. Streams of screaming projectiles poured through the hot air, falling and bursting everywhere. Men and horses were torn limb from limb; caissons exploded one after another in rapid succession, blowing the gunners to pieces. No spot within our lines was free from this frightful iron rain. The infantry hugged close to the earth and sought every slight shelter that our light earthworks afforded. It was literally a storm of shot and shell that the oldest soldier there — those that had taken in almost every battle of the war — had not yet witnessed. That awful, rushing sound of the flying missiles, which causes the firmest hearts to quail, is everywhere.

Mulholland continued:

For an hour after the firing began our batteries replied vigorously and then ceased altogether, but the rebel shells came as numerous as ever. Then, for over a half hour, not a soul was seen stirring on our line — we might have been an army of dead men for all the evidence of life visible.

Although they did not receive the brunt of the Confederate attack, the men of the Irish Brigade were witnesses to the great assault. Mulholland recalled:

At this moment silence reigned along our whole line. With arms at 'right shoulder shift.' the divisions of Longstreet's corps moved forward with a precision that was wonderfully beautiful. It is now our turn and the lines that a few moments before seemed so still

now teemed with animation. Eighty of our guns open their brazen mouths; solid shot and shells are sent on their errand of destruction in quick succession. We see them fall in countless numbers among the advancing troops. Their accuracy of our fire could not be excelled; the missiles strike right in the ranks, tearing and rending them in every direction. The ground over which they have passed is strewn with dead and wounded. But on they come.

Nearly seventeen years after the battle, Mulholland wrote of the advancing Confederates with respect:

At Waterloo the Old Guard recoiled before a less severe fire. But there was no recoil in these men of the South — they marched right on as though they courted death. They concentrate in great numbers and strike on the most advanced part of our line. The crash of the musketry and the cheers of the men blend together.

An unknown New York soldier wrote of the great battle on July 30, 1863:

On the 3d of July, as they were laying behind the hastily thrown-up breastworks, preparatory to the renewal of the preceding day, our batteries being placed in the most advantageous position in rear of the infantry, we plainly saw by the commotion visible amongst the enemy that some daring move from their side was contemplated. And we had not long to wait, for soon we saw a long line of their skirmishers thrown out with the evident intention of attacking our works; the main body soon made their appearance, and the whole column advanced against us in fine order, in close column of their brigades, but when they reached good open ground our artillery poured into them at short range canister and shot, and it was terrible to see the fearful gaps that would be made in their ranks at every discharge of our cannon.

In less than an hour it was over. The Federal line had been breached for a short time, but the gallant Confederates could not maintain their position on Cemetery Ridge. Those who were not captured, killed, or wounded drifted back across the open field, only to be met by a sorrowful and defeated Robert E. Lee saying, "It's all my fault."

In less than twenty-four hours the Irish Brigade had lost 198 men out of 532 engaged.

Private in Captain Thomas Francis Meagher's Zouave Company of the 69th New York State Militia at the Battle of Bull Run.

Major St. Clair A Mulholland at the battle of Chancellorsville.

War mementoes of St. Clair Mulholland. Clockwise from upper left: a watch fob made from a bullet which wounded Mulholland, blood stained officer's sash, Colonel's shoulder straps, Medal of Honor presented for action at the battle of Chancellorsville, and a Brigadier General's star. *Mulholland Collection, CWLM.*

Private, 28th Mass. Volunteer Infantry at the battle of Fredericksburg.

Lieutenant-Colonel Dale was hit in the side, the ball cutting away his undershirt but not breaking the skin. Lieutenant Cosslett was shot in the forehead, the ball cutting through his cap and making a deep flesh wound along the scalp. A young boy, Daniel Chisholm, had the front of his cap shot away, but leaving him unhurt; and so many a close call was talked about before, as one by one, the tired soldiers sank to rest in the blood-drenched woods.
— *St. Clair A. Mulholland*
The Story of the 116th Regiment Pennsylvania Volunteers in the War of the Rebellion

"...WE RUN THIS MACHINE NOW."

Although the men of the Irish Brigade had been severely tested at Gettysburg, they remained resolute in their determination to honorably and gallantly do their duty. The war continued with the passing of the Army of Northern Virginia and Army of the Potomac across the Potomac River and into Virginia.

St. Clair A. Mulholland recalled an incident on September 15, 1863, which was typical of the skirmishes between the two great armies:

The useless firing across a river indulged in by most of the army was never relished by the men of the Irish Brigade, who thought it sheer nonsense to blaze away and keep everybody from enjoying rest and comfort without accomplishing the slightest result. An effort was made at once to have the firing cease and cook supper. Captain Granger, of the Eighty-eighth New York, jumped from cover, waved his sword and stuck it in the ground. The Southern boys understood the signal and, inquiring 'what troops.' found it was the Irish Brigade. A picket truce followed immediately and all hands settled down to boil their coffee in peace, while for miles to the right and left the useless fusillade was continued far into the night.

In a letter dated near Centreville, Virginia, October 16, 1863, a veteran of the 88th New York wrote of the battle of Bristoe Station:

On the 14th we were shelled at breakfast by the advance of the enemy, fought six hours in retreat, capturing the first battery by a coup de main, encountered them ten miles further on at Bristoe Station, fought, with two divisions, the whole of A.P. Hill's corps, held our position till after midnight, Irish Brigade last, alone and unsupported, till the others were safe at a distance, then a double-quick for twelve miles, crossing Deep Run and Bull Run, where we halted, a march of 76 miles in 56 hours, fighting two severe engagements in one day, and having to guard the entire baggage and reserve artillery of the army. This is unprecedented in the annals of war, beating the famous march of the Fifty-second to Talavera. We captured two colors, five guns and four hundred and fifty prisoners, and lost nothing.

In his history of the Brigade, D.P. Conyngham wrote of the Mine Run campaign, in November, 1863:

As the corps were at breakfast that morning, they first felt the immediate proximity of the enemy, whose shot and shell came ploughing through the advanced ranks, formed of the Fifty-second N.Y.V., 'a conscript regiment,' the men of which wavered and fell back on the old commands.

As this occurred, Colonel Frank, who commanded the Third Brigade, rode in their front and rallied them, crying out, 'Stand, boys! follow me!.' Beyond them was the Second Brigade — or Irish Brigade — who cooly stood to their guns. Colonel Miles, too, rallied the lines. In a moment the panic subsided and the men stood cooly in their lines, though the shot and shell of the enemy were knocking them over pretty fast. Here my horse and some men beside me were killed by a shell. The lines now fell back behind the crest of the hill, and Ricketts' Battery having taken position, returned the enemy's killing compliments with interest.

In the late-fall of 1863, as the Irish Brigade settled into winter quarters, north of the Rapidan River, they could assess the trials of the previous year. Having been engaged in three major campaigns and numerous small battles and skirmishes, their ranks had been decimated by nearly half.

The early months of 1864 were spent in recruiting replacements for the obliterated ranks of the Irish Brigade.

The Brigade's next great test came in the dark tangled undergrowth known as "the Wilderness" on May 5th and 6th. In his history of the Brigade, D.P. Conyngham described the action of the 6th:

All day long the contest raged with little intermission, till towards evening, when the hardest fighting of the campaign commenced, the rebels sweeping

Captian Pierce Ryder, 88th New York Infantry, killed at the battle of the Wilderness, 5 May 1864.
Roger Hunt Collection, USAMHI.

down on Hancock in four imposing lines. Before these advancing waves of our skirmishers slowly retired to the front line of our defences, where our men awaited the onset; when within musket-range, the enemy opened a vigorous fire on our men, who replied with fatal effect, until Longstreet's forces were so severely handled that the reserves were ordered up. The contest was thus kept up for nearly an hour, when, in one position of the line, near where the wilderness had been set on fire and our breastworks had been demolished, the rebels pushed in with a shout of anticipated victory, and planted their colors on our works.

In his regimental history, St. Clair Mulholland described the fire which broke out in the tinder dry woods:

The fight was short and sharp. The men replied vigorously for a few moments, then the breast-work, which was built up with dry fence rails and logs, caught fire. The wind fanned the flames, and soon the whole line in front of the Regiment was in a blaze. The smoke rolled back in clouds; the flames leaped ten and fifteen feet high, rolled back and scorched the men until the heat became intolerable, the musket balls the while whistling and screaming through the smoke and fire. A scene of terror and wild dismay, but no man in the ranks of the Regiment moved an inch.

Mulholland continued:

How many poor, wounded souls perished in the flames none but the angels who were there to receive their brave spirits will ever know; but the very

awfulness of the situation seemed to call forth renewed evidence of courage and, when volunteers were demanded to rescue the wounded, Lieutenant Cosslett and a score of noble men rushed into the smoke and fire to save them.

Less than a week later the Army of the Potomac again faced the Army of Northern Virginia, near the quiet hamlet of Spotsylvania Court House in a running battle that lasted nearly two weeks. In his history of the Brigade, Conyngham described some of the early successes of the Second Corps:

Next morning (12th) the contest was renewed at dawn, Hancock opening the battle with such determined activity that by eight o'clock he had routed the best troops of the rebel army, among them the Stonewall Division, led by General Ewell, capturing three generals, thirty guns, and several thousand prisoners (four thousand, I think). Then the rebels massed their troops against him in such numbers that he found it difficult to retain the advantage gained, and the Sixth Corps was sent to his assistance. Thus, about eleven o'clock A.M. the battle raged with undiminished fury in Hancock's front, until dusk; was renewed at nine P.M., and continued until nearly three A.M., both parties contending during the night for the possession of a line of rifle-pits from which Hancock had driven the enemy in the morning. The rebels fell back at length, and our men followed them steadily through the woods, skirmishing as they advanced for a distance of nearly four miles, when Lee took up new position.

Three days later, with the support of the their Irish brothers in the Corcoran Legion, the

Irish Brigade participated in a gallant assault against the heavily entrenched Confederate position. Conyngham wrote:

At last the field is crossed, the rebels fly from their first intrenched (sic) position, and our men clamber over, cheerily, capturing a few dilatory sharpshooters who lingered too long at their post. Again they charge after the retreating but still fighting foe; and the line is not quite as orderly as might be desired, owing to the unevenness of the ground, which was in various places covered with dense pine-woods. But the veterans of the Second Corps, unmindful of the driving tempest of bullets, shot, and shell, reformed their disordered ranks, pushed steadily on, and soon took possession of the second line of fortifications.

St. Clair Mulholland recalled the famous hand-to-hand struggle which took place within the Confederate entrenchments:

The men of the One Hundred and Sixteenth were among the first over the works, and the colors of the Regiment were in advance. Personal encounters between individuals took place on every part of the disputed ground. Lieutenant Fraley, of Company F, ran a Confederate color-bearer through with his sword; a Confederate shot one of the men when almost within touch of his musket, then threw down his piece and called out, 'I surrender,' but Dan Crawford, of Company K, shot him dead; Billy Hager, of the same company, ran into a group of half a dozen and demanded their surrender, saying, 'Throw down your arms, quick now, or I'll stick my bayonet into you, and they

obeyed. Henry J. Bell, known as 'Binky Bell,' leaped over the works and yelled 'Look out, throw down your arms, we run this machine now.'

The Army of the Potomac continued its relentless pursuit of General Lee and his army, with the next great battle at Cold Harbor. At 4:30 a.m. the Federals began an assault against the Confederate position along a six-mile front which proved to be impregnable. Mulholland wrote in his regimental history:

No sooner had the attacking party begun moving than the enemy opened

Colonel Richard Byrnes, 28th Massachusetts Infantry. Byrnes died 3 June 1864 of wounds received at the battle of Cold Harbor. *Meade Album, CWLM.*

fire, and a terrible and destructive fire it was, sweeping the ground in all directions. The Irish Brigade was in the second line, but soon caught up with those in front and joined in the fray. The Confederates were found strongly posted in a sunken road in front of their works, from which they were driven after a severe fight and followed into their works. Three hundred prisoners, one color and three pieces of artillery were captured in the first rush, but the victory was quickly turned into a most disastrous defeat.

Mulholland continued:

Colonel Richard Byrne (Twenty-eighth Massachusetts Infantry), commanding the Irish Brigade, was mortally wounded and died in the field hospital, where he had lingered for a few days....He was strict, reserved and reticent and one who did not know him would think him severe, but he was a man who did his full duty and expected everyone else to come up to the full measure of all demands. To those who knew him best he was kindly and lovable. A few days before the battle he had some words with Captain Lieb, then commanding the One Hundred Sixteenth, and may have been a little harsh in his remarks, but, when borne to the field hospital and learning that Lieb was there also, he had himself carried to where the Captain was lying and the dying officer apologized in the most courteous manner for anything rude that he might have said.

The regimental flags were of deep rich green, heavily fringed, having in the centre a richly embroidered Irish harp, with a sunburst above it and a wreath of shamrock beneath. Underneath, on a crimson scroll, in Irish characters, was the motto, 'They shall never retreat from the charge of lances.' …The staff-mountings were silver-plated; the top being a pike-head, under which was knotted a long bannerol of safron-colored silk, fringed with bullion, and marked with the number of the regiment.

—D.P. Conyngham
The Irish Brigade

PEACE

In the last ten months of the war, the Irish Brigade saw many changes, including being consolidated with another brigade and being re-formed as the Second Irish Brigade. Throughout, however, the resolve of the men who fought and died next to the flag of Erin never waned.

Following the surrender of the Army of Northern Virginia at Appomattox Court House on April 9, 1865, the two armies met peacefully for the first time in nearly four years. In his history of the Brigade, D.P. Conyngham wrote:

Victors and vanquished then mingled freely together; rations of all kinds were issued to the half-famished Confederates, and the rest of the afternoon of this eventful day was spent in deeds of kindness and mutual rejoicing that the end had at last been reached, and peace was to reign once more.

After participating in the Grand Review in Washington, D.C. on May 24, the Irish Brigade returned home. The New York Times reported on July 4:

The famous and now long-tried Irish Brigade, under the command of

Captain Garrett Nowlen, 116th Pennsylvania Infantry, killed at the battle of Reams' Station, 26 August 1864. Nowlen was postumously promoted to Major to date from his death. *USAMHI*

Brevet Brigadier General Robert Nugent, arrived early yesterday morning, remaining all of yesterday and last night at the Battery, preparatory to taking part in the grand celebration of today. This brigade consists of four regiments, viz: the Sixty-third, Sixty-ninth, and Eighty-eighth New York, and the Twenty-eighth Massachusetts Regiment, from Boston. The brigade has an extensive and gallant record, having shared in the glory of every engagement fought by the army of the Potomac, since its organization, from the siege of Yorktown and the Peninsula campaign, under McClellan, through all the different campaigns of Hooker Burnside, Meade and Grant, down to the final surrender of the army of northern Virginia, under Lee, at Appomattox Hollow, Va., April 9, 1865.

As the wounds of war healed, the men of the Irish Brigade gathered on their former fields of battle to honor their comrades who gave their all for their adopted country. Although the last survivor of the Brigade died long ago, their deeds of valor are preserved in private collections and museums, in the words they wrote, the monuments they dedicated to their comrades, and with the tattered flags they followed into so many battles.

At the dedication the Irish Brigade monument at Gettysburg, Denis F. Bourke said:

> *Comrades we have seen these two banners wave at Gaines' Mill when despair and defeat were imminent; they*

Colonel Robert Nugent and officers of the Irish Brigade, probably taken in June, 1865. Note mourning badges worn by the officers on their left sleeves. *Mass. MOLLUS Collection, USAMHI.*

waved at Malvern Hill when the ground shook beneath the charging legions of Lee; we have seen them at Antietam breast the shock of death, when their folds became as gory as the ground over which we bore them, and, though reddened and stained with the smoke and blood of battle, they still maintained their position in the front. They waved together here when a Continent was at stake; they flashed in the Wilderness amid a revel of death; they were the first flags planted on the angle at Spotsylvania; and at each and every place, begirt by patriotism and battalioned by valor, they never wavered, never faltered, never quailed until they blazed in the sunlight of victory at Appomattox.

"None but the brave deserve the fair."

— Quote often heard in Irish Brigade camps.

IN CAMP, FIELD, AND HOSPITAL

Over the years, the men of the Irish Brigade have acquired the somewhat erroneous reputation of being a hard drinking rabble of undisciplined fighters. Father William Corby, in his **Memoirs of Chaplain Life**, described the men and officers of General Meagher's brigade:

> *The officers of his command were, for the most part, men of superior education, gallant beyond any around them in the army; and as for bravery, this they imbibed with their mother's milk, yea, it was born in them. The 'rank and file' was composed of healthy, intelligent men, far above the average, and in many cases of liberal education.*

At the dedication of Irish Brigade monuments at Gettysburg, Colonel James J. Smith described the men of the 69th New York:

> *It was a cheerful regiment, playing cards under fire, joking while actually engaged in file firing, and in camp ready for anything from a snowball fight to tossing pie peddlers in blankets, or driving a mule in full uniform into the Colonel's tent....*
> *They were a well drilled regiment, with clean brasses and muskets, even if they hadn't been able to wash for a week. They had no idea of being second to any other in anything.*

Heavily retouched photo of Private William Tighe.
New York State Adjutant General's Collection, USAMHI.

Because the men of the Brigade were predominantly Roman Catholic, the service of chaplains was particularly noticed and appreciated. In his history of the 116th Pennsylvania Infantry, St. Clair Mulholland remembered:

Seldom was an obscene word or an oath heard in the camp. Meetings for prayer were of almost daily occurrence, and the groups of men sitting on the ground or gathered on the hill side listening to the Gospel were strong reminders of the mounds of Galilee when the people sat upon the ground to hear the Saviour teach. Oft times in the Regiment the dawn witnessed the smoke of incense ascend to heaven amid the templed trees where series groups knelt on the green sod and listened to the murmur of the Mass.

Father William Corby wrote:

At no time during the war from the organization of the brigade till after the 'surrender of Lee,' was it without a priest; and men from various sections of the army, during the active campaign, when they needed the services of a priest, directed their steps to the Irish Brigade, where they were sure to find one. To this brigade, as a rule, were the generals also referred, when a priest was needed to assist men sentenced to death by court-martial.

The 63rd New York Infantry in the field. Note the regimental band and officers in the foreground.
Army of the Potomac Albums, CWLM

But all was not seriousness and piousness in the Irish Brigade camps. One of the most famous incidents occurred on St. Patrick's Day, 1863. In his History of the Philadelphia Brigade, Charles Banes wrote:

The officers had their amusements as well as the men, and General Meagher of the Irish Brigade arranged a celebration of St. Patrick's day that was suited to all tastes. The general, dressed as a master of hounds, instituted hurdle-races, pole-climbing matches, and a variety of field sports, closing the performance with a complimentary dinner to the Second Corps officers. Unfortunately for some of us who were present, the general did not succeed in accommodating all guests. He extricated himself from the difficulty, however, as gallantly as he went into the charge at Marye's Heights, by saying, 'Gentlemen, if you do not all succeed in finding seats at the table, please remember that Thomas Francis Meagher's hospitality is not as large as his heart.

Among the greatest dangers faced by any soldier was duty along the picket line. Irish Brigade historian Conyngham wrote:

Perhaps picket duty is more full of scenes and incidents than any other of the numerous duties of the soldier. The hostile pickets are most likely separated by some open valley. The men sit at the foot of tall trees, or sheltered behind a clump of wood, gazing intently, trying to see their enemy through the dense forest branches. Only a few hundred yards off are the Confederate pickets, watching just as intently. The least little indiscretion, the least noise, and you attract the keen gaze of your enemy, and quick as lightening a bullet is aimed at you.

But the picket line also allowed fraternization with the enemy. Conyngham recalled:

Perhaps the men of the Irish Brigade lived on better terms with the enemy than the others. Oftentimes, when the rebel pickets were firing on our men, they would cease as soon as the Brigade relieved the others, and a most friendly feeling would soon spring up, and a regular barter of coffee, sugar, whiskey, and tobacco take place.... The canteen would be emptied, old times and friends discusses, as the little party seated themselves under the shelter of some clump of trees between both lines.

St. Clair Mulholland recalled a humorous incident at the battle of Spotsylvania Court House:

No matter how terrible the surroundings in a fight, there seemed to be a ludicrous incident sure to pop up and cause a smile. One of these was when Robert Glendenning, of Company K, had his wig carried away by a passing shell, and the boys thought his head was gone, but he turned up all right, though very bald.

All too often, however, battle was a serious business which was revealed in the horrors of hospitals. Historian Conyngham described one hospital scene:

It looks like a perfect butcher's shambles, with maimed and bloody men lying on all sides; some with their arms off; some with their legs off; some awaiting their turn; while the doctors, with

44

upturned cuffs and bloody hands, are flourishing their fearful knives and saws around, and piles of raw, bloody-looking limbs are strewn around them: while some who have died on the dissecting table, add to the ghastly picture.

Father William Corby also described the care of the wounded:

As soon as a general engagement begins, the wounded are carried back from the front so far as it is possible to do so. Many poor fellows must lie where they fall for several hours, and, in some cases, even for several days. This is especially the case when one army drives back the other, and in turn is driven

back itself, so that on the disputed ground between the two forces the wounded of both armies may be so situated that their comrades cannot reach them until a flag of truce be sent over. It is not easy to do this, especially at night; and sometimes the fighting may begin so early on the following morning that there is no chance to do so. Want of transportation, also, often keeps them in the same position. When the conditions are favorable, the wounded are carried back, and the surgeons, with others in command, determine upon a place of safety, and here is located the hospital.

Father Corby continued:

Officers of the 28th Massachusetts Infantry. Doctor Peter E. Hubron, the regimental surgeon, sits second from left. *Mass. MOLLUS Collection, USAMHI*

Unique four-piece collapsible drinking cup carried by Dr. Peter E. Hubron while a surgeon of the 28th Massachusetts Infantry. *Courtesy of David Hann.*

When amputation was to be made (and this took place after every battle), the victim was placed on a table, or some boards in that shape, chloroform was administered, then the knife and saw made 'short work' of a man's leg or arm. You might see outside the quasi-hospital, in one great pile, legs, arms, hands, and feet, covered with the fresh blood of the owners — a scene that would sicken most persons to such an extent as to make them hope never to see the like again.

D.P. Conyngham also remembered the horrible scenes of the hospitals:

The shifting lights of the lamps as the doctors passed from sufferer to sufferer, the stifled cries and groans, the shriek if agony and despair that burst from the lips of some, smote sadly on the heart; and as the morning broke, the trees shattered by shot and shell, broken caissons and guns, the dead and dying men and animals around, were sad traces of war.

Undoubtedly the saddest trace of any battle were the thousands of fresh graves which would appear in peaceful farmer's fields. Father Corby described the gruesome task of burying the dead:

The usual way is not to dig a grave for each man, but a long pit about six and a half feet wide and deep enough to hold all the dead in the immediate vicinity. The bodies are placed side by side and on top of each other in the pit, which is then covered over much the same as farmers cover potatoes and roots to preserve them from the frost of winter; with this exception, however: the vegetables really get more tender care.

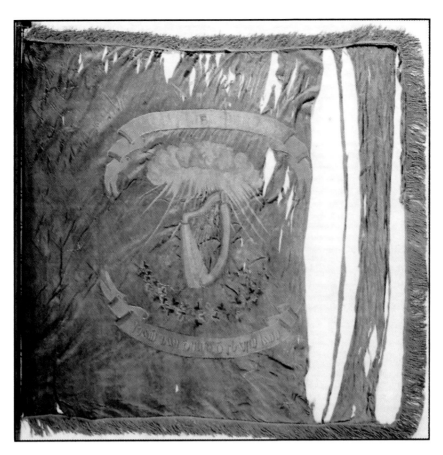

1st model Irish color. *Courtesy of Ken Powers*

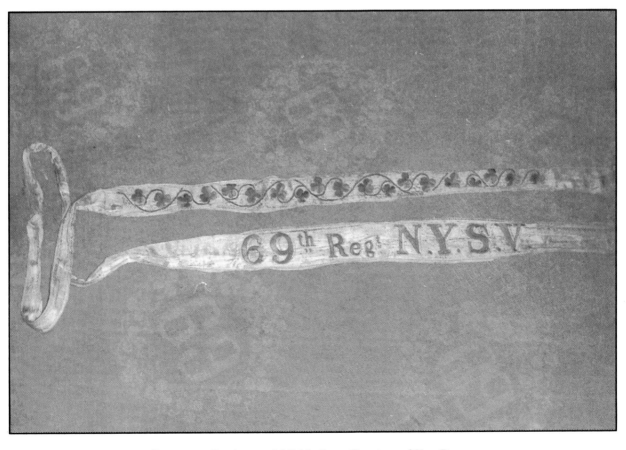

Streamers for 1st model Irish flag. *Courtesy of Ken Powers*

Symbolism and the Irish Flag

The first Irish flags, made by Tiffany, were presented to the New York regiments of the Irish Brigade by a committee of Irish ladies in November, 1861. For the rest of the war, the New York regiments and the 28th Massachusetts would be irrevocably linked with the green flag of Erin. (The 116th Pennsylvania Infantry did not carry the green flag.)

As with many colors of the period, these flags were rich with symbolism. The harp is the Brian Boro harp, the only king of a united Ireland, who was killed at the battle of Clontarf in 1014. The shamrocks symbolize Ireland and her Christianity, while the sunburst is a symbol seen primarily in American Fenian societies. Below the sunburst and harp is the motto, *"Riam Nar Druid O Sbairn Lann"* ("Who never retreated from the clash of lances"), which has its origin in Irish mythology.

Officers and color party of the 63rd New York. Flags left to right: State Regimental, National Colors, and Secord Model Irish Brigade. *USAMHI*

CONFEDERATE GENERALS OF IRISH BIRTH

WILLIAM MONTAGUE BROWNE

Born in Dublin in 1823, Browne served in the Crimean War in an English regiment before settling in the United States in 1851. At the outbreak of the war he was appointed a colonel of cavalry and served on the personal staff of Confederate President Jefferson Davis. The Confederate President appointed Browne temporary brigadier general on November 11, 1864; a nomination which was rejected by the Confederate Senate the following February, although Browne was paroled as a brigadier general at the end of the war.

Major General Patrick Ronayne Cleburne, Confederate States Army. *Meade Album, CWLM*

PATRICK RONAYNE CLEBURNE

The son a prominent physician, Cleburne was born on March 17, 1828, ten miles west of Cork. After serving in the Forty-first Regiment of Foot, he emigrated to the United States in 1849, finally settling in Helena, Arkansas. A successful druggist and lawyer, he organized the Yell Rifles, which he led in the successful capture of the Little Rock Arsenal.

Named colonel of the First Arkansas Infantry, he later assumed command of the Fifteenth Arkansas and was promoted to brigadier general on March 4, 1862. At the battle of Shiloh, in April, 1862, Cleburne's brigade was initially repulsed, but rallied under the general's command to push through the Federal camps. Cleburne saw further action at Perryville, and was shot through the cheek at Richmond, Kentucky on August 30, 1862. Promoted to major general the following December, Cleburne gained the reputation as one of the most tenacious generals the Confederacy had, often being called "the Stonewall Jackson of the West." He fought gallantly at Murfreesboro, Chickamauga, Chattanooga, the

Atlanta Campaign, and was given the thanks of the Confederate Congress when he saved Braxton Bragg's artillery train at Ringgold Gap. Cleburne entered the political arena when he became one of the first Confederate officers to suggest that freed slaves be used as soldiers.

Loved by his men and respected by his peers, Cleburne was known for his gallantry in action. At the battle of Franklin, Tennessee, November 30, 1864, Cleburne had two horses shot from under him in the advance against the Union line. Raising his kepi on the end of his sword, he led the advance on foot before being killed within fifty yards of the enemy line.

WALTER PAYE LANE

Born in County Cork, February 18, 1817, Lane was brought to the United States at the age of four. Raised in Ohio, Lane led an incredible life of adventure prior to the war; fighting at the battle of San Jacinto, serving as a Texas Ranger during the Mexican War, as a crewman on a privateer, fighting Indians, and mining in California, Arizona, Nevada, and Peru.

As lieutenant colonel of the Third Texas cavalry, Lane saw action at Wilson's Creek, Pea Ridge, Corinth, and was severely wounded at the battle of Mansfield, Louisiana in April, 1864. His appointment to brigadier general was approved by the Confederate Senate on March, 17, 1865, the last day that body met.

JOSEPH FINEGAN

Born in Clones, Ireland on November 17, 1814, Finegan moved to Florida in his twenties and was a member of the state secession convention in 1861. In April, 1862 he was commissioned brigadier general and placed in command of the District of Middle and East Florida. Charged with defending the thinly manned Florida coast, Finegan commanded the Confederate forces in the battle of Olustee in February, 1864. Transferred to the Army of Northern Virginia, where he led a brigade of Floridians, Finegan's troops successfully repulsed three separate attacks at the battle of Cold Harbor on June 3, 1864. He remained with the Army of Northern Virginia until being recalled to Florida in March, 1865.

UNION GENERALS OF IRISH BIRTH

RICHARD BUSTEED

Born February 16, 1822, in Craven, Ireland, Busteed organized a battery of independent light artillery in October, 1861, but resigned his commission as captain a month later. On August 7, 1862, he was appointed brigadier general of volunteers, and in September, 1863 was appointed judge for the U.S. District Court for Alabama.

PATRICK EDWARD CONNOR

Born on March 17, 1820, in County Kerry, Ireland, Connor received his first military service in the Seminole and Mexican Wars. In September, 1861 he accepted a commission as Colonel of the Third California Infantry and was given command of the District of Utah, headquartered at Fort Douglas near Salt Lake City. He received a promotion to brigadier general after defeating the Bannock and Shoshone Indians, and because of his success in keeping the mail route open to California. Connor was later presented with the honorary rank of brevet major general.

MICHAEL CORCORAN

Born in Carrowkeel, County Donegal, Ireland, on September 21, 1827, Corocoran was the son of a British Army captain. In 1845, at the age of 18, Corcoran was appointed in the Irish constabulary but resigned in 1849, protesting harsh measures taken against his countrymen. Upon emigrating to the United States in 1849, Corcoran continued his military career by enlisting as a private in the 69th New York State Militia. Promoted to colonel in 1859, Corcoran refused to parade his regiment during a parade in honor of the visiting Prince of Wales. Court-martial charges against Corcoran were dropped upon the outbreak of the war and he led the regiment at the battle of First Bull Run, where he distinguished himself, was wounded and captured.

Controversy followed Corcoran as a Confederate prisoner when he became a victim of a diplomatic scheme played between the United States and Confederate governments. (When the Federal government threatened capital punishment to the crews of captured privateers, the Confederate government theatened like treatment to a high-ranking Union prisoners. Corcoran became one of the high-ranking officers through a lottery. His life was spared when the privateer crews were declared prisoners of war.) Exchanged in August, 1862, Corcoran was promoted to brigadier general of volunteers to date from the battle of First Bull Run.

Corcoran then organized a brigade comprised, of the 155th, 164th, 170th, and 182nd New York Regiments, known as the Corcoran Legion. Assigned to the Seventh Corps, Department of Virginia, in November, 1862, the brigade saw action in North Carolina and southeastern Virginia before being transferred to the Department of Washington. Corcoran rose to divisional command in October, 1863.

Tragically, while riding near Fairfax Court House, Virginia with Brigadier General Thomas Francis Meagher, Corcoran was crushed to death when his horse fell on him. He died on December 21, 1863, and was buried in Calvary Cemetery, Long Island City, New York.

WILLIAM GAMBLE

Born in County Tyrone, on January 1, 1818, William Gamble became a civil engineer before moving to the United States at the age of about twenty. In 1839, he enlisted in the First Dragoons and rose to the rank of sergeant major. After being honorably discharged in 1843, Gamble worked as a civil engineer until he accepted a commission as lieutenant colonel of the Eighth Illinois Cavalry in September, 1861. The following December, Gamble became the regiment's colonel.

Gamble was wounded in the chest at Malvern Hill, July 1, 1862, and did not rejoin his regiment until the battle of Fredericksburg that December. In January, 1863, Gamble was given command of a cavalry brigade.

Gamble's greatest test came during the early morning hours of July 1, 1863, when the fate of the nation rested in the hands of a relatively few Union cavalrymen. On a dusty road west of Gettysburg, Pennsylvania, Brigadier General John Buford's division, of which Gamble's brigade was a part, met a Confederate division advancing toward the small crossroads town. Although badly outnumbered, the Federal cavalrymen were able to slow the Confederate advance for nearly two hours, allowing Union forces to come from the rear and thus preventing a Confederate victory on the first day of the battle.

In May, 1864 Gamble was given command of a cavalry division, and was breveted brigadier general of volunteers the following December.

Gamble was mustered out of service as brigadier general of volunteers, but continued to serve in the army as a major in the Eighth U.S. Cavalry. While traveling to California, Gamble contracted cholera and died in Nicaragua on December 20, 1866.

RICHARD HENRY JACKSON

Born at Kinnegad, County Westmeath, on July 14, 1830, Jackson enlisted in the Fourth U.S. Artillery in 1851, rising to the rank of captain in the next eleven years. Jackson held a number of commands throughout the war, including chief of artillery of the Tenth Army Corps and commander of the Second Division of the all-black Twenty-fifth Corps. After the war, he was breveted brigadier and major general of volunteers, as well as brevet brigadier general in the regular army.

PATRICK HENRY JONES

Born in County Westmeath, in 1830, Jones gave up his lucrative New York law practice to become a second lieutenant in the Thirty-seventh New York Infantry, "The Irish Rifles." Eventually rising to the rank of colonel of the One Hundred Fifty-seventh New York Infantry Regiment, Jones saw action during the Peninsula campaign and Second Manassas, and was severely wounded and taken prisoner at the battle of Chancellorsville. Jones returned to his unit in time to participate in the attack on Missionary Ridge, Tennessee on November 25, 1863. In June,

1864, Jones was given brigade command and on April 18, 1865 was promoted to brigadier general of volunteers to rank from the previous December.

JAMES LAWLER KIERNAN

The son of a British navy surgeon, Kiernan was born October 26, 1837, at Mount Bellew, County Galway. After studying in Dublin, Kiernan graduated from New York University Academy of Medicine at the age of nineteen. Kiernan served as an assistant surgeon with the Sixty-ninth New York State Militia at the battle of First Bull Run. After moving west he served as surgeon of the Sixth Missouri Cavalry and saw action at the battle of Pea Ridge.

After this, Kiernan's military service becomes somewhat sketchy, with one account saying that he became tired of medical service. Kiernan reportedly accepted a position as major of the regiment, was shot through the lung, left for dead in a swamp, captured, and escaped. He did resign as surgeon of the Sixth Missouri in May, 1863, and was commissioned brigadier general of volunteers on August 1. Kiernan commanded a post at Miliken's Bend, Louisiana, but resigned because of poor health in February, 1864.

MICHAEL KELLY LAWLER

Born in County Kildare, on November 16, 1814, Lawler served in the Mexican War and saw action at Vera Cruz and Mexico City.

Lawler returned to the military and was mustered into federal service with the Eighteenth Illinois Infantry in the spring of 1861. Wounded during the assault on Fort Donnelson, in May, 1863, he was promoted to brigadier general to rank from the previous November. During the Vicksburg campaign, he commanded a brigade at Port Gibson and led one of the most successful federal assaults of the war, capturing more than 1,100 Confederates. Lawler served the remainder of the war in various commands throughout Louisiana and Texas, and commanded the Division of East Louisiana at the end of hostilities. On March 13, 1865, he was breveted major general of volunteers and was mustered out in 1866.

JAMES SHIELDS

Born in County Tyrone, on May 10, 1810, Shields served in the Blackhawk War before becoming involved in democratic politics and law. Because of a newspaper criticism, Shields challenged a political opponent to a duel. The problem was resolved when the offending party, one Abraham Lincoln, provided an explanation. Afterwards Shields and Lincoln became close friends. Sheilds served as a brigadier general of volunteers during the Mexican War, was wounded at Cerro Gordo, and was breveted major general.

Appointed brigadier general of volunteers from California, Shields commanded a division during the Valley campaign with little accomplishment. He resigned his commission in March, 1863 to accept a position with a railroad in San Fransisco.

THOMAS FRANCIS MEAGHER

Born in Waterford, Ireland, August 3, 1823, Thomas Francis Meagher was educated at an Irish Jesuit school and an English college before becoming active in the Irish independence movement. Arrested by British authorities, Meagher was banished to Tasmania in 1849, fled to the

Brigadier General Thomas Francis Meagher, Irish revolutionary, who formed the Irish Brigade. *Mass. MOLLUS Collection, USAMHI*

United States in 1852, eventually settled in New York, and became a respected spokesman in the Irish independence movement.

In 1861, he organized a company of Zouaves which became part of the 69th New York State Militia, under the command of Michael Corcoran. After the 69th N.Y.S.M. was mustered out of Federal service, Meagher organized the famous "Irish Brigade" and was promoted to Brigadier General of volunteers in February, 1862. After gallantly leading his brigade through several bloody battles, Meagher was refused permission to recruit to fill its decimated ranks. He resigned his commission as of May 14, 1864, but the resignation was not accepted and was refused the following December.

Meagher was given several positions within Major General William T. Sherman's army, including command of the Georgia Department of Etowah and "Meagher's Provisional Division." Again dissatisfied with his assignments, Meagher resigned on May 15, 1865, while stationed in Savanah, Georgia.

Meagher's excellent military accomplishments were rewarded with an appointment as territorial secretary of Montana, in which he served as acting governor for more than a year.

Like his close friend Michael Corcoran, Meagher died tragically during a drinking bout at Fort Benton, Montana. Meagher mysteriously fell from a steamboat and drowned in the Missouri River. His body was never recovered.

THOMAS ALFRED SMYTH

Born in County Cork, on December 25, 1832, Smyth emigrated to the United States at the age of twenty-two. After spending time in Philadelphia, he joined William Walker's expedition to Nicaragua, after which he settled in Wilmington, Delaware, as a coachmaker.

At the outbreak of the war Smyth offered a company of infantry to the state of Delaware, but the company became part of the all-Irish Twenty-fourth Pennsylvania Infantry, a ninety day regiment. After being mustered out of the Twenty-fourth, Smyth accepted a commission as major of the First Delaware Infantry, and was given command of the regiment in February, 1863. Smyth led his regiment at the battles of Antietam, Fredericksburg, and Chancellorsville. At the battle of

Gettysburg Smyth commanded the Second Brigade, Third Division of the Second Army Corps. In March, 1864, Smyth was assumeded temporary commander of the Irish Brigade, a position he held until Colonel Richard Byrnes returned to the command. Promoted to brigadier general of volunteers in October, 1864, Smyth rose to divisional command.

Known for his bravery and coolness under fire, Smyth could often be found riding beyond his picket lines, causing many of his men to comment that he led a charmed life. During the action near Farmville, Virginia, on April 7, 1865, Smyth was shot by a sharpshooter, the ball entering his mouth and shattering his spine. He died two days later, on April 9, the same day that Robert E. Lee surrendered the

Army of Northern Virginia. The last Federal general killed in the war, Smyth was posthumously promoted to brevet major general, to date from the day of his wounding.

Brigadier General Thomas A. Smyth, who died of wounds 9 April 1865, just hours before Lee's surrender at Appomattox Court House, *Mass. MOLLUS Collection, USAMHI*

THOMAS WILLIAM SWEENY

Born in County Cork, on December 25, 1820, Sweeny lost an arm at the battle of Churubusco, during the Mexican War, but was rewarded with a brevet promotion and a silver medal presented by the City of New York. Sweeny remained in the army, reaching the rank of captain in the Second United States Infantry Regiment by the outbreak of the Civil War.

Sweeny was wounded commanding a regiment of Missouri militia at Wilson's Creek and while commanding a brigade at Shiloh. After recovering from his second wound, Sweeny resumed brigade command at the battle of Corinth and was promoted to brigadier general in March, 1863, to date from the previous November. After spending time in garrison duty, Sweeny led a division at Snake Creek Gap, Resaca, Kenesaw Mountain, and Atlanta.

After the war, Sweeny became involved with the Fenian invasion of Canada, an attempt to conquer Canada in order to free Ireland. He was released after being arrested by United States authorities and despite a reputation as a rebel, was placed on the retired list with the rank of brigadier general in May, 1870.

IRISH BRIGADE MEDAL OF HONOR RECIPIENTS WHO WERE BORN IN IRELAND

Private Timothy Donoghue
Company B, 69th New York Infantry
Fredericksburg, VA, 13 December 1863
Was wounded while voluntarily rescuing a
wounded officer from between the lines.

First Lieutenant George Ford
Company E, 88th New York Infantry
Sailors Creek, VA, 6 April 1865
Capture of an enemy flag.

Major St. Clair A. Mulholland
116th Pennsylvania Infantry
Chancellorsville, VA, 4-5 May 1863
While in command of the picket line, held
the enemy in check all night to cover the
retreat of the Army of the Potomac.

Private Peter Rafferty
Company B, 69th New York Infantry
Malvern Hill, VA, 1 July 1862
After being wounded and directed to the
rear, remained in action and sustained
several more wounds, resulting in his
capture and total disability for military
service.

St. Clair A. Mulholland as a Brevet - Brigadier
General *Mass. MOLLUS Collection, USAMHI*

OTHER IRISH-BORN MEDAL OF HONOR RECIPIENTS

Sergeant Major Augustus Barry, 16th U.S. Infantry
Sergeant Terrance Begley, 7th New York Heavy Artillery
Private Felix Branagan, 74th New York Infantry
Sergeant John Brosnan, 164th New York Infantry
Private Michael Burk, 125th New York Infantry
Private William Campbell, 30th Ohio Infantry
Sergeant Hugh Carey, 82nd New York Infantry
Private David Casey, 25th Massachusetts Infantry
Private James Connors, 43rd New York Infantry
Private Thomas Cosgrove, 30th Massachusetts Infantry
Private John Creed, 23rd Illinois Infantry
Corporal James Cullen, 82nd New York Infantry
Corporal Patrick Doody, 164th New York Infantry
Private William Downey, 4th Massachusetts Cavalry
Private Thomas Fallon, 37th New York Infantry
Corporal Christopher Flynn, 14th Connecticutt Infantry
Sergeant Richard Gasson, 47th New York Infantry
Private Patrick Ginley, 1st New York Light Artillery
Lieutenant James Gribben, 2nd New York Cavalry
Sergeant John Havron, 1st Rhode Island Infantry
Corporal Patrick Highland, 23rd Illinois Infantry
Assistant Surgeon Bernard Irwin, U.S. Army
First Sergeant Patrick Irwin, 14th Michigan Infantry
First Sergeant William Jones, 73rd New York Infantry
Corporal John Kane, 100th New York Infantry
Sergeant Major Joseph Keele, 182nd New York Infantry
Private Thomas Kelly, 6th U.S. Cavalry
Private John Kennedy, 2nd U.S. Artillery
Corporal John Keough, 67th Pennsylvania Infantry
Captain John Lonergan, 13th Vermont Infantry
Private Richard Mangum, 148th New York Infantry
Corporal Peter McAdams, 98th Pennsylvania Infantry
Lieutenant Charles McAnally, 69th Pennsylvania Infantry
Private Bernard McCarren, 1st Delaware Infantry
Sergeant Patrick McEnroe, 6th New York Cavalry
Corporal Owen McGough, 5th U.S. Artillery
Sergeant Thomas McGraw, 23rd Illinois Infantry
Private Patrick McGuire, Chicago Mercantile Battery, Illinois Light Artillery
Corporal Alexander McHale, 26th Michigan Infantry

Color Sergeant Gerorge McKee, 89th New York Infantry
Private Michael McKeever, 5th Pennsylvania Cavalry
Corporal Patrick Monaghan, 48th Pennsylvania Infantry
Sergeant Dennis J.F. Murphy, 14th Wisconsin Infantry
Private John Murphy, 5th Ohio Infantry
Corporal Thomas C. Murphy, 31st Illinois Infantry
First Sergeant Thomas J. Murphy, 146th New York Infantry
Sergeant John Nolan, 8th New Hampshire Infantry
Private Peter O'Brien, 1st New York (Lincoln) Cavalry
Private Timothy O'Connor, 1st U.S. Cavalry
Private George C. Platt, 6th U.S. Cavalry
Private Thomas Riley, 1st Louisiana Cavalry
Private John Robinson, 19th Massachusetts Infantry
Private Thomas Robinson, 81st Pennsylvania Infantry
Private Peter Ryan, 11th Indiana Infantry
Private Patrick Scanlon, 4th Massachusetts Cavalry
Private Timothy Spilane, 16th Pennsylvania Cavalry
Private Bernard Shields, 2nd West Virginia Cavalry
Private Joseph Stewart, 1st Maryland Infantry
Sergeant William Toomer, 127th Illinois Infantry
Corporal George Tyrell, 5th Ohio Infantry
Private M. Emmett Urell, 82nd New York Infantry
Corporal John Walsh, 5th New York Cavalry
Corporal Richard Welch, 37th Massachusetts Infantry
Chief Bugler Thomas Wells, 6th New York Cavalry
Private Edward Welsh, 54th Ohio Infantry
Private James Welsh, 4th Rhode Island Infantry
Private Christopher Wilson, 73rd New York Infantry
Private Robert Wright, 14th U.S. Infantry

NOTE: It is possible that other Irish-born soldiers were recipients of the Medal of Honor, but are not listed as their place of birth was not noted by the War Department.

Source: <u>The Medal of Honor of the United States Army</u>, Washington: Government Printing Office, 1948.

BIBLIOGRAPHY

BOOKS

Banes, Charles H. <u>History of the Philadelphia Brigade</u>. Philadelphia, J.B. Lippincott & Company, 1876. (Reprinted by Butternut Press, Gaithersburg, Maryland, 1984.)

Bates, Samuel P. <u>Martial Deeds of Pennsylvania</u>. Philadelphia: T.H. Davis and Company, 1873.

Boatner, Mark Mayo III. <u>The Civil War Dictionary</u>. New York: Davis McKay Company, Inc., 1959.

Busey, John and David G. Martin. <u>Regimental Strengths and Losses at Gettysburg</u>. Hightstown, N.J.: Longstreet House, 1986.

Cavanaugh, Michael. <u>Memoirs of Gen. Thomas Francis Meagher, Comprising the Leading Events of His Career Chronologically Arranged, With Selections From His Speeches, Lectures and Miscellaneous Writings, Including Personal Reminiscences</u>. Worcester, Mass.: The Messenger Press, 1892.

Conyngham, David P. <u>The Irish Brigade and its Campaigns</u>. New York: William McSorley & Company, 1867. (Recently reprinted by Olde Soldier Books, Inc. of Gaithersburg, Maryland.)

Corby, William. <u>Memoirs of Chaplain Life by Very Rev. W. Corby, C.S.C. of Notre Dame University, Indiana</u>. Chicago: La Monte, O'Donnell & Co., Printers, 1893.

Lonn, Ella. <u>Foreigners in the Union Army and Navy</u>. Baton Rouge: Louisiana State University Press, 1951.

Mulholland, St. Clair A. <u>The Story of the One Hundred and Sixteenth Regiment Pennsylvania Volunteers in the War of the Rebellion; the Record of a Gallant Command</u>. Philadelphia: F. McManus, Jr. & Company, Printers, 1903.

New York Monuments Commission for the Battlefields of Gettysburg and Chattanooga. <u>Final Report on the Battlefield of Gettysburg</u>. 3 volumes. Albany: J.B. Lyon Company, Printers, 1900.

Pennsylvania. Gettysburg Battlefield Commission. <u>Pennsylvania at Gettysburg. Ceremonious at the Dedication of the Monuments Erected by the Commonwealth of Pennsylvania to Mark the Positions of the Pennsylvania Commands Engaged in the Battle</u>. 2 volumes. Edited by John P.

Nicholson. Harrisburg: E.K. Meyers, State Printer, 1893.

Walker, Francis A. History of the Second Army Corps in the Army of the Potomac. New York: Charles Scribner's Sons, 1886. (Recently reprinted by Olde Soldier Books, Gaithersburg, Maryland.)

Warner, Ezra J. Generals in Blue: Lives of the Union Commanders. Baton Rouge: Louisiana State University Press, 1964.

Warner, Ezra J. Generals in Gray: The Lives of the Confederate Commanders. Baton Rouge: Louisiana State University Press, 1959.

The Medal of Honor of the United States Army. Washington: Government Printing Office, 1948.

The War of the Rebellion: A Compilation of the Official Records of the Union and Confederate Armies. 128 volumes. Washington: Government Printing Office, 1889.

MANUSCRIPT AND PHOTOGRAPHIC COLLECTIONS

Army of the Potomac Albums, The Civil War Library and Museum, Philadelphia, PA. Meade Album, The Civil War Library and Museum, Philadelphia, PA.

Newspaper Files, Division of Military and Naval Affairs, Albany, New York.

St. Clair A. Mulholland Collection, The Civil War Library and Museum, Philadelphia, PA.

NEWSPAPERS

Contemporary and post-war newspapers, containing many articles and letters written by Irish Brigade members, were extremely helpful in this study. Unfortunately, many of the articles appeared as clippings in scrapbooks with no notations made as to the author or even the source newspaper. Among the newspapers which were particularly useful, where the source was known, were:
The New York Leader
The New York Times
The Philadelphia Hibernian
The Philadelphia Inquirer
The Philadelphia Times

MAGAZINES

Civil War line art from Century Magazine.